SESAME STREET®

Love the Earth Crafts

I ❤ trash!

First published by Parragon in 2009

Parragon
Queen Street House
4 Queen Street
Bath BA1 1HE, UK

ISBN 978-1-4075-3808-2

Printed in China

123

SESAME STREET®

Love the Earth

Crafts

I ♥ trash!

PaRragon

Bath • New York • Singapore • Hong Kong • Cologne • Delhi • Melbourne

Contents

This book is full of creative, fun things to make for your family, your friends and yourself for all kinds of occasions.

Tips for Parents and Caregivers

This book is for the whole family. Its primary purpose is to bring together parents and children, from preschoolers to teens, to have fun making things! True, making things with young children can take time and get a little messy. But it will be fun and it will give them a sense of achievement. Once children start making things, they just might become "crafters" for life.

The Importance of Doing Crafts with Children

The projects that appear in this book were designed for, worked on, and tested by young children and their families. Every craft project in this book highlights at least one task that a young child can perform. Make sure to choose projects with steps that you think your own child can accomplish with relative ease. Remember, what seems like a small, simple task to you—applying glue to the back of a piece of paper, coloring in a simple design, or arranging shells in a dish—is a big accomplishment for a small child, and can instill a sense of pride.

From the time a child picks up his first crayon until he reaches adulthood, he goes through several developmental stages with regard to arts and crafts—from scribbles (about age 2), to assigning meaning to shapes drawn (about age 5); to the creation of three-dimensional objects (about age 8.) Although the pace at which each child progresses may differ, important skills can be developed by working with crafts.

Learning Skills

- Logic, problem solving
- Basic math skills (measuring; using a ruler; using measuring cups)
- Reading (looking at directions or reading a recipe)
- Following sequential directions
- Creativity and artistic sensibility
- Self-esteem and a sense of uniqueness
- Fine and gross motor skills
- Eye-hand coordination
- Cleaning skills (including responsibility)
- Fun!

How to Use This Book

The crafts included here all require the supervision (and usually the hands-on help) of an adult, especially with preschool-aged children. However, each craft contains at least one "kids!" icon (featuring a *Sesame Street* character) indicating a step that your preschooler should be able to accomplish, depending on the skills and abilities of your individual child. Also included with each craft are special features written for the children that bring "words of wisdom" (or just fun thoughts!) from the *Sesame Street* friends.

The first step in creating each craft is to read through the directions for the project from beginning to end. That way you and your child will know what materials and tools you will need. If she is able, encourage her to read familiar numbers out loud from the materials list, and pick out her favorite letters of the alphabet. Although understanding written fractions can be difficult for preschoolers, you can certainly point out "½" in a materials list and explain the concept of "one half" by showing her that if you cut one whole pipe cleaner into two equal parts, you now have two halves.

Finally, although directions for these crafts are often quite specific in order to ensure clarity, remember that part of the fun of making crafts is to be creative. We encourage you to experiment with color, found objects, or decorating in any way that seems appropriate and appealing. Don't worry if the end result doesn't look exactly like the photo. Half the fun of crafting is developing your own style and expression.

A Few Thoughts on Safety

1 Avoid accidental choking. It's natural for very young children to put small objects, such as beads, magnets, and crayons, into their mouths. Please supervise your child, no matter what age, at all times. Make it very clear that none of these materials belong in the mouth, then keep a watchful eye.

2 Keep away from hot or sharp objects. When making your crafts in the kitchen, be sure you are working at a safe distance from a hot stove and sharp objects, such as knives.

3 Tie back long hair; roll up sleeves. Both you and your child should wear an apron, or old clothes, since they might get spattered with glue or paint.

4 Clean up before and after working with crafts. Start with a clean work surface so your materials will stay clean. After you've finished, clean up thoroughly.

5 Work slowly and carefully. Just do one step at a time.

Get crafty

It's a good idea to keep all your craft materials together. You can design a special craft box, or purchase an inexpensive plastic container from an office supply or container store. Create a special craft "work space" (if you have the space) and cover it with a plastic or paper tablecloth, newspaper or other protection as you work.

Essential Tools

Here's a useful list of essential tools and materials you'll need to do most of the projects in this book.

- Scissors (those with rounded tips are safest for younger children)
- A set of acrylic paints in basic primary colors (red, blue, yellow, black and white)
- Paintbrushes in various sizes and thicknesses
- White glue and an old paintbrush to apply it
- Colored pencils; colored markers; crayons
- Black fine-tipped felt pen
- Pencils
- Ruler
- Large eraser

More useful materials

Here are some other materials you might want to have on hand. Look out for things to collect or interesting materials to store at home until you are ready to craft. This is a great way to reuse things and make less trash in the world.

Gift wrap

Recycled gift wrap can come in handy for many projects. If it's too crumpled, iron it with a cool iron, and it will be as good as new.

Cardboard

Use recycled cardboard from packing boxes, cereal boxes, laundry detergent boxes, or other cardboard packages to make your projects.

Fabric

Worn out blue jeans can be turned into bags, purses, and pencil cases. Scraps of patterned fabric can be used to make bean bags, pouches, as a covering for boxes, or as decorations in infinite ways.

Odds and ends

Save odd buttons, earrings, and other old jewelry in cookie tins, then use them as craft decorations. Even old bottle caps (both metal and plastic) can be used in creative ways.

Objects from nature

When you are outdoors in the park or garden, pick up pretty leaves, interesting twigs, feathers, pine cones, seed heads, stones, and other objects from nature. At the beach collect shells, pebbles, and driftwood.

Useful Recipes

Papier-mâché recipe

Papier-mâché is a light, strong molding material made from newspaper (or other paper) and pulped with glue and water. Many different recipes are available, but this one is the easiest.

1 If you want to make a bowl (or any shape), you can cover a balloon with papier-mâché or wrap layers of papier-mâché around a real bowl of the size you wish. If you use a real bowl, smear petroleum jelly over it before you begin to apply the papier-mâché so that the model will slip off easily when it is dry.

You will need
- Newspaper, torn into short strips
- Dish of white glue, mixed with an equal amount of water
- Paintbrush

2 Using a paintbrush, paint the strips of newspaper with the glue mixture. Place the strips one at a time over the object and smooth them down with your hands. Add one layer at a time. Don't put too many layers on at once or the paper will take too long to dry.

Salt dough recipe

Salt dough is an inedible molding material that's easy to make and can be used in many different craft projects.

1 Using your fingers, mix together the flour, salt, and cooking oil in a bowl. Add a little water and mix it in thoroughly until you have a smooth, thick dough, dry enough not to stick to the sides of the bowl. If your mixture is too sticky, simply add more flour; if it's too crumbly, add water.

You will need
- ¾ cup all purpose flour
- 3 tablespoons salt
- 1 teaspoon cooking oil
- ⅓ cup water
- Mixing bowl
- Board

2 Sprinkle a little flour over the board and knead the dough until it is a smooth lump. You can store the dough in a sealed container in the refrigerator for up to three days.

3 Mold your designs. Bake them in a pre-heated oven at 250°F for about 3 hours until firm. Baking times will vary depending on the size and thickness of your object, but make sure it's hard all through.

Tips for success

1 Prepare your space

Cover your workspace with newspaper or a plastic or paper tablecloth. Make sure you and your children are wearing clothes (including shoes!) that you don't mind becoming spattered with food, paint, or glue. But relax! You'll never completely avoid mess; in fact, it's part of the fun!

2 Wash your hands

Wash your hands (and your child's hands) before starting a new project, and clean up as you go along. Clean hands make for clean crafts! Remember to wash hands afterwards too, using soap and warm water to get off any of the remaining materials.

3 Follow steps carefully

Follow each step carefully, and in the sequence in which it appears. We've tested all the projects; we know they work, and we want them to work for you, too. Also, ask your children, if they are old enough, to read along with you as you work through the steps. For a younger child, you can direct her to look at the pictures on the page to try to guess what the next step is.

Fishy glitter globe

This is a great way to use an old jar. Fill it with glittery water, paint on your favorite fish, like Dorothy, and shake up a storm!

You will need

- Empty round jar and lid
- Seashells (optional)
- All-purpose waterproof glue
- Black relief outliner glass paint
- Glass paints: red, orange, green
- Paintbrush
- Water
- Glycerine
- Blue glitter

1

Arrange shells on the inside of the jar lid. Glue them to the lid and let dry.

2

Turn the jar upside down and, using the black relief paint, draw the outline of fish and seaweed. Let dry.

3

Using the glass paints and brush, color in the seaweed and fish, blending the paints together. Let dry.

4 Fill the jar with water. Add a teaspoon of glitter and a few drops of glycerine.

5 Put a line of glue around the lid and screw it tightly to the top of the jar. Let dry overnight.

Glycerine is great! It makes the water thicker, so when you shake the jar, the glitter falls slowly to the bottom. You can buy it in the home-baking department of your supermarket.

Shake the jar and place it upside down to give your fish a glittery sea to swim in.

Fabulous flower pot

Flowers come in all shapes and sizes, and some of them smell so pretty. Make a special pot to keep your favorite bunch of flowers in.

You will need

★★ Flower-patterned gift wrap or
★★ Pictures of flowers from magazines
★★ White glue and brush
★★ Plastic flowerpot

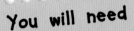

1

Cut out the prettiest flower shapes from the gift wrap or magazines.

2

kids

Brush glue around the outside of the plastic flowerpot.

3

Glue the cut-out flowers to the flowerpot. Overlap them to make a pretty pattern.

Brush a thin layer of glue over the cut-outs to make the pot waterproof.

You can decorate some pots with pictures of different leaves, or butterflies, or anything else you like. Elmo likes it when butterflies land on flowers. When did you last see a butterfly?

Bird feeder

Recycling is a good way to use old things in a new way. For example, turn an old juice carton into a bird feeder.

You will need

- Empty, rinsed-out juice carton with a nozzle
- Sandpaper
- Scissors
- Acrylic paints
- Paintbrush
- Bird seed
- Garden wire
- Mesh netting bag
- Varnish

1

Rub the outside of the carton with sandpaper until it's rough. Cut out a rectangular hole on the side facing away from the nozzle.

kids 2

Paint the carton all over in one color. This one is brown to look like tree bark.

kids 3

After the paint is dry, add different shades and colors. This one has knots and vines, just like bark.

4

Add leaves or other decorations in a different color. When you've finished painting, add a coat of varnish to help protect the feeder during cold and wet months.

5

Fill the mesh netting bag with birdseed, then push it through the rectangular hole in the feeder. Remove the nozzle, then pull the top of the bag through the spout. Next, thread wire through the top of the bag and twist the ends together. Hang the feeder up outside.

That's so magic—the old juice carton is now a bird feeder!

Pebble porcupines

Elmo likes making animals from smooth beach pebbles. Elmo is painting pebble porcupines today. What will you paint?

You will need

- 1 large and 2 small smooth stones
- Acrylic paints
- Medium and small paintbrushes
- Clear varnish

kids 1

Wash and dry the stones. Paint them the color of the animal you want to make. Paint an extra coat if you need to. Let dry.

Asking questions is a good way to find out about something you want to know. Like... what is a porcupine? You'll find the answer in step 2.

2

Porcupines are animals with spiky spines or quills. To make pebble porcupines, paint the pebbles gray, let dry, then paint on black bristles.

3

Now add a nose and two eyes, then paint your other pebbles.

4

If your pebbles are going to live outside on your doorstep or your backyard, give them all a coat of clear varnish.

Elmo has made a scaly fish friend for Dorothy from this long pebble. Elmo is looking in his animal book to see what other creatures he can make from his pebbles.

Garden on a plate

Making a miniature garden will keep you busy on a rainy day. Collect tiny cuttings of shrubs and flowers from the backyard and get planting!

You will need

- Old dinner plate
- Soil mix
- Moss, grass, and small flowers, e.g. daisies
- Cuttings from shrubs
- Fir tree twig
- Aluminum foil
- Old jar lid
- 2 twigs and length of string
- Paper and colored pencils
- Scissors
- Small pebbles

1

Put a ¼ inch layer of soil mix on the plate. Press moss into about three-quarters of the area.

2

Put small pebbles around the plate edge and make a path of pebbles in the soil, as shown.

3

Push a fir twig into the soil to make a miniature tree. Then push the flowers, shrubs, and grass into the soil.

4

Mold aluminum foil around an old jar lid to make a pond. Cut out a paper circle to fit in the bottom of the lid. Color it blue, and draw some goldfish onto it. Put some more blades of grass around the pond to look like reeds.

kids 5

Draw some clothes on a piece of white paper, giving them tags so you can hang them on the washing line. Color them and cut them out.

6

Make a washing line from the twigs and string. Hide two small pieces of plasticine in the moss and push the twigs into them. Glue the clothes to the line.

Spritz your garden with water to keep it fresh. Replace the flowers when they begin to wilt.

Starry pen tube

Make a tube to hold pens, pencils, or crayons for yourself or give it as a gift. This one is designed like the night sky with stars and comets.

1

You will need

- Cardboard tube with lid
- Fine sandpaper
- Black acrylic paint
- Paintbrush
- White glue and brush
- Glitter: gold, silver
- Scrap paper
- Sequins and star stickers

Lightly rub the tube all over with sandpaper. This will help the paint stick better to the tube.

kids 2

Cover the tube in black acrylic paint. Let dry, then apply another coat. Let the can dry thoroughly.

kids 3

Brush some glue onto the tube then sprinkle the glitter over the top. Shake off the excess glitter onto a piece of scrap paper.

4

Add the star stickers. Glue a row of sequins around the top and bottom of the tube, or anywhere to make your pen tube shimmer.

Stars shine brightly at night. I love to look up at the stars. They're so beautiful!

Birdseed wreath

Elmo wonders if his friend Big Bird will like this natural "birdfeeder." Elmo thinks it looks delicious!

1

With a spoon, spread peanut butter over one side of the bread ring.

You will need

- A loaf of ring-shaped bread
- Peanut butter
- Spoon
- Birdseed
- Shallow dish or plate
- Baking sheet
- Length of ribbon

2

Pour birdseed into the dish, then dip the peanut-butter side of the bread ring into the seeds.

3

Bake in the oven for 10 minutes at 425°F.

4

When the bread is cool, tie a ribbon around the top and hang it in your backyard from a nearby tree.

This will be grea... winter when it's ha... birds to find f...

STUFF

Bottle skittles

Play skittles in the backyard or, if it's raining, indoors. Roll a ball at the skittles and try to knock as many over as you can.

You will need

- 6 identical clear plastic drinks bottles with lids
- Ready-mixed paints: red, yellow, green
- Dishwashing liquid
- Old jug
- Self-adhesive star and planet stickers
- Funnel
- Sand
- Ball

1

In an old jug, mix the green paint with water until it looks like soup. Add a small squirt of dishwashing liquid.

kids 2

Pour some paint mixture into a bottle and put the top on. Shake the bottle to spread the paint all over the inside of the bottle. Add more paint if you need to.

kids 3

Remove the top, pour out any remaining paint and let the bottle dry. Repeat for the other bottles, making three red, two green, and one yellow skittles.

Put the funnel in the neck of the bottle and pour in sand until half full. This makes the skittles harder to knock over. Repeat for each of the bottles.

Put the tops back tightly on the bottles. Decorate the skittles with self-adhesive stickers.

Painting the skittles from the inside of the bottle means the paint won't chip when you play with them.

Cactus garden

It's so easy to grow a cactus garden. A sunny windowsill and some water once a week are all these prickly plants need.

You will need

★★ 5 small assorted cacti
★★ Stone bowl large enough for all 5 cacti
★★ Cactus soil mix
★★ Wad of paper towels
★★ Old spoon
★★ Colored gravel or sand

1

Put a thin layer of gravel in the bottom of the bowl. Add soil mix almost to the top of the bowl. Make a hole in the soil mix with your finger.

2

Fold the paper towels around the tallest cactus and remove it from its pot. Put it in the hole you have made and push down the soil mix firmly all around it.

3

Make another hole in the soil mix and plant the second tallest cactus in the same way as before.

Continue planting. Use an old spoon to press down the soil mix firmly around the base of each cactus.

Using the spoon, arrange the gravel around the base of each cactus until the soil mix is covered.

If you don't have colored gravel, make a desert garden instead by spreading sand on top of the soil mix.

Designer shoes

Use a clean pair of canvas shoes or sneakers for this craft, and personalize them with your own pictures and patterns.

1

Use the paint to draw and color pictures on your sneakers. Here are scary skulls. Boo! Let dry.

You will need

- Pair of clean sneakers or canvas shoes
- Fabric paints
- Fabric pens
- Glitter
- Plastic gemstones
- Beads

2

Next, add some more detail in a different colored paint, like these flames. Let dry.

3

Once you've finished your design on both shoes, leave them to dry thoroughly.

Sometimes the paint shrinks a little as it dries and flakes off. Touch up with some fresh paint if needed.

Now you're ready to wear your totally unique footwear.

I've given my ballet slippers a pretty princess look, by gluing glitter and plastic gemstones onto the shoes, then drawing patterns with the fabric pens. Finally, I threaded beads onto the laces.

Sand butterfly

Elmo is a very busy monster. Elmo is painting a butterfly picture using sand. What will you paint with sand?

You will need

- 8 × 11 inch sheets of cardboard
- 8 × 11 inch sheets of white paper
- Pencil
- Black felt-tip pen
- Scissors
- 11¾ × 16½ inch sheet scrap paper
- White glue and brush
- Colored sand: red, orange, yellow, blue, green
- Teaspoon

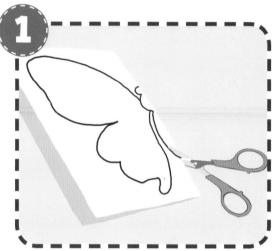

1

To make a butterfly, fold the white paper and draw half of its shape on one side. Cut it out. Unfold the shape and put it on the cardboard at an angle.

2

Use the black felt-tip pen to draw around the outline. Add butterfly markings, matching the pattern on each wing.

3

Place the scrap paper under the cardboard. Paste a thin layer of white glue over the butterfly's body and head only.

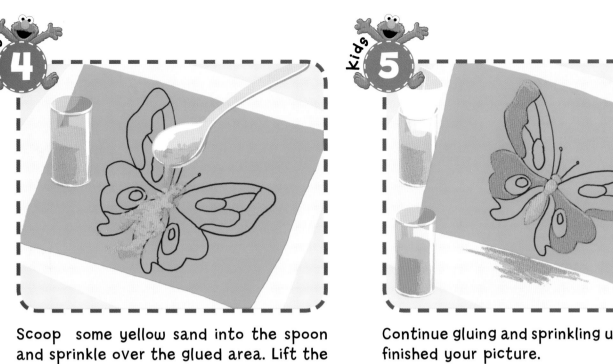

Scoop some yellow sand into the spoon and sprinkle over the glued area. Lift the picture and gently tap the spare sand onto the scrap paper. Carefully pour the sand back into its container.

Continue gluing and sprinkling until you've finished your picture.

It is I, Grover, your furry adorable globe trotter. I traveled all the way to Italy. Did you know "farfalle" is butterfly-shaped pasta?

Flower garland

My mommy helped me make this colorful garland. It's a necklace made of flowers. It's so magic!

You will need

★ 80 sheets of tissue paper in 2 different colors (40 of each) cut into squares of 8 × 8 inches
★ Bag of pipe cleaners
★ Length of elastic or ribbon
★ Scissors

1

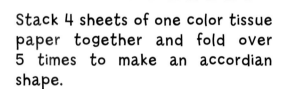

Stack 4 sheets of one color tissue paper together and fold over 5 times to make an accordian shape.

2

Cut both ends into a round shape then twist a pipe cleaner around the middle. Don't trim the ends of the pipe cleaner.

3

Gently separate out the tissue paper on both sides of the pipe cleaner into a flower shape.

4

Twist the ends of the pipe cleaner around the ribbon or elastic and make sure the ends are not sticking out. Keep adding flowers until your garland is done.

Nonny is Hawaiian. She told me that Hawaiians make flower garlands called "leis" as a sign of love and friendship.

Veggie print shirt

Me don't just eat food. Me can use food for other things, such as making a hand-printed T-shirt like this one.

You will need

- Clean white T-shirt
- Piece of scrap cardboard
- Vegetables: 1 large potato, 1 small potato, 1 stalk of celery, 1 carrot
- Cutting board and knife
- Fabric paint (green or color of choice)
- Shallow dish
- Tube of fabric relief paint (metallic blue or color of choice)

1

Cut the two potatoes in half and trim the top of the celery. Cut a 1¼ inch piece of carrot; then cut it in half lengthways.

kids 2

Place cardboard inside the shirt to stop the paint from seeping through. To make the frog's body: dip a large potato half into the paint, and print it in the center of the T-shirt.

kids 3

Use one of the small potato halves to print the two back legs. Dip the top end of the celery stalk into the paint and use to print his bulging eyes.

4

5

Use the carrot to print the lower back legs and the front legs, then cut the carrot piece in half to print the front and back feet. Let dry.

Dab tiny spots all over the frog, using the tube of fabric paint. Let the T-shirt dry thoroughly.

This cute gecko was also made with potato, carrot, and celery, with yellow relief paint dotted over its body. Can you think of any other animal shapes you can make with vegetables?

Papier-mâché bowl

Balloons are great for making bowls. After the papier-mâché dries, just pop the balloon to leave a perfect bowl shape!

You will need

- Balloon
- Torn newspaper strips
- White glue, brush and water
- Scissors
- Masking tape
- Round plastic lid
- White latex paint and brush
- Ruler and pencil
- Set of acrylic paints
- Water-based varnish and brush

kids 1

Blow up the balloon. Make the papier-mâché from the recipe at the start of this book. Glue papier-mâché strips halfway up the balloon. Repeat with 3 layers.

2

When the papier-mâché is dry, pop the balloon and remove it. Trim the edges of the bowl by cutting around the rim until it's smooth and even.

kids 3

Sit the bowl in the plastic lid and tape them together. Paste 2 more layers of papier-mâché over the whole model and let dry.

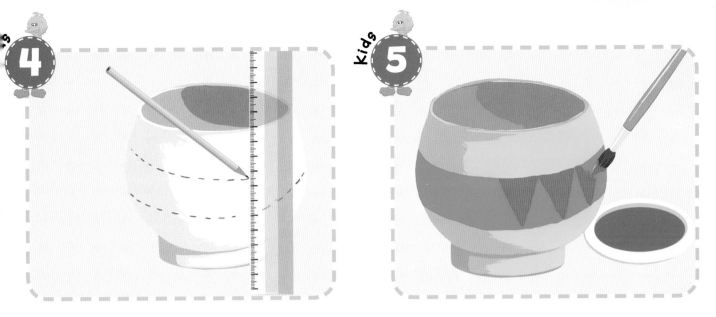

Paint the bowl all over, including the inside, with a coat of white latex paint. Let dry. Hold the ruler beside the bowl and mark 2 straight lines of dots around the bowl. Join the dots to make lines.

Paint on a striped pattern in bright colors and let dry. Add spots, triangles, or other designs. Let dry, then add a thin coat of varnish to make the bowl tough and shiny.

It's important to let the papier-mâché dry completely before you pop the balloon or start painting. If it is still soft and damp, you could easily put your finger through it and that would ruin your bowl!

Striped coin saver

The Count has made this striped coin saver. Use an empty potato chip can. Start saving your spare money and you'll be filthy rich before you know it!

You will need

- Empty cardboard container with lid
- Ruler and pencil
- Several 8½ x 11 inch sheets of colored paper
- White glue and brush
- Craft knife or box cutter

1

Measure the height of the container and cut the paper to the same height. Draw narrow and wide lines down one sheet.

2

Put the ruled sheet with the lines drawn on it on top of the others and cut along the lines to make long strips.

kids **3**

Paint the strips with glue and stick them to the can, making sure they overlap and smoothing them down carefully.

4

After the glue has dried, cut a slot measuring about 2 x ¼ inches.

Animal boots

Elmo can't play outside when it's raining. But when it stops, Elmo keeps his furry feet dry in these fun boots.

You will need

- Old newspaper
- Plain-colored rubber boots
- Felt-tip pen (thin tip)
- Acrylic paint and paintbrush
- Tubed glitter glue
- Googly eyes
- White glue and brush

Kids

1

Stuff newspaper into the boots so they stay firm. Using the felt-tip pen, draw some shapes on them.

2

Paint the bigger areas with paint. Let dry. Add another coat of paint if necessary.

3

Carefully squeeze out the glitter glue into whatever shapes you like. Add more paint, if necessary.

4

Glue the googly eyes onto the boots. Let dry in a warm, dry place.

For me, I love yucchy rainy days. What's your favorite kind of weather?

ABBY CADABBY

Leaf creatures

These leaf creatures look so funny and they're easy to make. You just need some leaves and some imagination.

kids

1

Choose a large dried leaf and glue it onto the piece of cardboard.

You will need

- ✦ Various dried leaves
- ✦ Piece of cardboard (any color)
- ✦ White glue and brush
- ✦ Colored pens
- ✦ Colored paper
- ✦ Scissors
- ✦ Googly eyes, or colored dot stickers

kids

2

Choose some smaller leaves and stick them to the cardboard for hands, feet, and ears. Draw lines between the small leaves and the big leaf for arms and legs.

3

Stick googly eyes onto the leaf and add a smile shape cut from the colored paper.

Make more leaf creatures using different kinds of leaves. Make funny faces, like 3 eyes or curly antennae.

Elmo loves making leaf creatures best. Elmo is going to make up names for these leaf creatures. Do you want to try too?

Indoor garden

Make a plant pot for herbs, bulbs or seeds. This is my kind of mess.

You will need

- 3 yogurt containers
- Sandpaper
- Acrylic paints
- 3 carton lids
- Potted herbs, bulbs or seeds
- Soil mix
- Awl or screwdriver

kids

1

Wash and dry the containers and gently rub all over the outsides with sandpaper. This will help the paint to stick to the pots.

2

Make holes in the bottom of each pot with an awl or screwdriver.

Zoe's.

Brush two coats of paint on the outside of each pot. When the paint has dried, add a pattern, like these white dots, on each pot.

Paint some carton lids in bright colors to make matching saucers.

5

Remove the herbs, bulbs or seeds from their pots and repot them. Add extra soil to fill the pots. Press it down and water well.

Elmo added wobbly eyes and a smiley mouth to his plant pot. What other designs can you put on yours?

Printed star card

Rosita is helping me make this card out of paint, foam, and some thick cardboard. Do you want to have a go?

You will need

- Sheet of blue cardboard 6 x 12 inches, folded in half
- Tracing paper and pencil
- Scissors
- 3 pieces foam 2 x 2 inches
- 3 pieces thick cardboard 2 x 2 inches
- Acrylic paints: red, yellow, dark blue and a brush
- White glue and brush
- Red glitter

1

Glue a foam square onto a square of thick cardboard to create a stamp. Add yellow paint and print 5 squares in the corners and middle of the blue card. Let dry.

2

Draw a star onto the tracing paper. Trace the shape onto the foam to make 2 stars. Cut out.

3

Stick each star to a square of thick cardboard. Add blue paint to one of the star stamps and print a star onto each blue square.

4

Use the other star stamp to print red stars on the yellow squares. Let dry.

5

Mix a little water with glue and brush it onto the middle, top left, and bottom right red stars. Sprinkle red glitter over the glued stars and shake off any excess glitter. Let dry.

Greeting cards are given to celebrate a special time with someone. In Mexico, the country where I was born, we speak Spanish. "Feliz Cumpleaños" means Happy Birthday!

Alpine rock garden

Alpines are the very small plants that can be planted in gravel or pebble gardens. They need to be outdoors because they usually grow on mountain slopes.

You will need

★★ Alpine plants
★★ Plastic plant container
★★ Pebbles or stones
★★ Sand
★★ Trowel
★★ Gravel mix

1 Put some pebbles in the bottom of the container and use the trowel to fill it half way with sand.

2 Leave the plants in their pots and arrange them on top of the sand. Then add some more sand around the pots to hold them in place.

3 Place a thick layer of gravel over the sand and the pots but leave the plants sticking out of the top. Put some pebbles or stones on top of the gravel.

Water the gravel regularly to keep the plants moist.

Wow! This rocky garden looks beautiful.

Friendship bracelet

Show your best friend how much you like them with this great friendship bracelet.

You will need

❀ 4 strands of cotton thread: 2 mauve, 1 pink and 1 purple (or the colors of your choice), each 20 inches long
❀ 1 large bead and 4 medium-sized beads

1

Take the 4 strands of cotton thread and knot them together, 8 inches from one end.

kids

2

Thread the large bead on the bracelet and push it up as far as the knot.

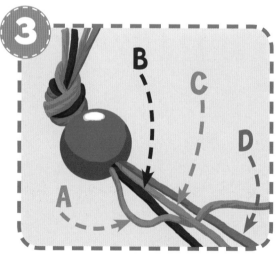

3

Spread out the 4 strands so that the 2 mauve strands are first and third from the left. Put A over B, under C, and over D. Pull A gently to tighten the weave.

4

Continue weaving B over C, under D and over A, working over, under, over, under. Pull gently to tighten before starting on the next left-hand strand.

5

Continue weaving until you are about 3 inches from the end, then tie the knotted strands into a knot, leaving the ends loose.

6

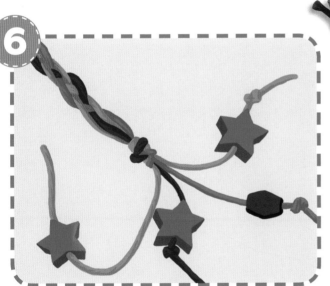

Thread a medium-sized bead onto each of the 4 loose strands and tie a knot to keep it in place.

I'm going to give my friendship bracelet to Zoe. She is coming over to my house to play. Who will you give your bracelet to?

Cress caterpillar

Watercress only takes a few days to grow and it tastes great in salads and sandwiches, too. Elmo loves watercress!

You will need

- 5 egg shells
- Nail scissors
- Paints: green, red, black
- Googly eyes
- Paintbrush
- White glue and brush
- Packet of watercress seeds
- Cotton batting
- Red pipe cleaner
- Water

1

Take 5 clean, empty egg shells with their tops cut off. Trim the top of the egg shells with nail scissors to make them smooth.

2

Paint the shells green. Glue googly eyes on one shell and paint a mouth. Put all the shells in an egg carton to dry.

kids 3

Once dry, place some cotton batting in the bottom of each shell. Add 1 teaspoon of watercress seeds and a spoonful of water to each shell.

4

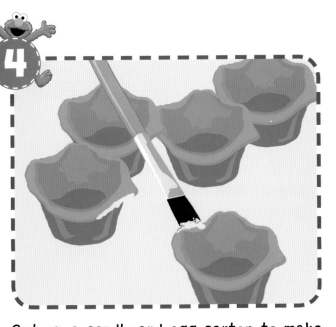

Cut up a cardboard egg carton to make five little dishes. Paint them green and glue them together in a wiggly line.

5

Place an egg shell in each dish, with the face at the front. Make antennas by twisting a pipe cleaner into spirals at both ends, fold it in half, then push it into the shell with the face.

Add a little water every other day. Within a week, the watercress will grow. Then you can wash and eat it. I'm going to make a cress salad for my good friend, Snuffy.

Potpourri bag

This pretty scented bag is also called a "sachet." If you place it in your drawer, it will keep your clothes smelling sweet like flowers.

You will need

✹ Tray
✹ Lavender flowers
✹ Rose petals
✹ Thin fabric 4 x 12 inches
✹ Fabric glue
✹ Rubber band
✹ Colored ribbon
✹ Scissors
✹ Colored felt or fabric scraps
✹ Beads or sequins (optional)

1

Spread out the lavender flowers and rose petals on a tray and allow them to dry for a couple of weeks.

2

Glue along the long sides of the fabric. Fold in half to make a bag. Press the edges together. Let dry.

3

Place some of the dried flowers inside the bag and gather the top together with a rubber band, then tie the ribbon on top.

4

Cut out small shapes from fabric or felt and glue them onto the bag. Glue on beads or sequins for extra decoration.

That smells too sweet for Grouches! I'd much rather smell garbage!

Tiger paws

Turn old tissue boxes into wild feet, like these tiger paws—maybe even your favorite monster's feet from Sesame Street.

You will need

- 2 empty tissue boxes
- Acrylic paints
- Paintbrush and old sponge
- Black funky foam
- 10 double-sided adhesive tabs or tape
- Scissors
- White glue and brush

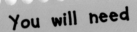

1 To make tiger feet paint the top and sides of the tissue boxes yellow, then let dry.

2 Dip a dry sponge in orange paint and dab it all over the boxes. Let dry.

3 Paint black stripes all over the boxes. Let dry.

4

Cut out claws from the black foam. Glue them onto the box using double-sided adhesive tabs on top.

Hey everybody. My feet are large and furry. What kind of feet will you make?

Animal nests

Nests are warm and safe homes for insects, and reptiles as well as for birds like Rubber Duckie and Big Bird. Make a cozy nest for your toy animals.

You will need

- Medium bag full of thin twigs
- Scissors
- White glue and brush
- Cardboard bowl
- Small brush

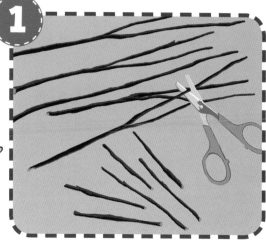

1 Cut the twigs into small pieces about 3-4 inches long.

2 Turn the cardboard bowl upside down and brush glue over the outside. Add a layer of twigs over the base and sides of the bowl wherever you spread the glue.

3 Brush glue around the inside of the bowl and add more twigs to the inside, until it looks like a nest.

4

Let dry for about one hour, then fill any gaps with more twigs and let dry.

Rubber Duckie likes nests, but he likes water too. Can you think of any other creatures that like water?

Pressed-flower card

Pressed flowers can be used to make beautiful greeting cards. Don't forget to check with an adult before you pick their favorite flowers!

You will need

★ Flowers and leaves
★ Heavy books (e.g. dictionaries)
★ Paper towels
★ White glue mixed with equal amount of water, and brush
★ Cream cardboard 16 x 18 inches
★ Scissors and ruler

kids

1

Pick some flower petals and leaves. Arrange them on paper towels, then put another piece of paper towel on top. Place them inside a book.

2

Place a pile of heavy books on top of the book with the flower, petals, and leaves inside. Leave them for at least two weeks.

3

Fold the cream cardboard in half and make a sharp crease with the point of the scissors and a ruler. Be careful not to cut the cardboard.

4

Remove the pressed petals and leaves from the book. Arrange them on the front of the card and glue them in position.

It might be ha[rd] to wait for the flowers to [be] ready—waiting is hard. Just think how much fun you'll have making the rest of the card when they're ready though. Can you remember another time you had to wait for something?

Sporty storage box

Even better than my trash can, this box is perfect for storing sports equipment. Or you could make a box for toys, art materials, or just your favorite things.

You will need

- Large cardboard box with lid
- Large and small paintbrushes
- Acrylic paints
- Pencil
- Paper
- Scissors
- White glue and brush

kids **1**

Paint the box and the lid in your favorite color. Leave to dry, then paint a second coat.

2

Draw different pieces of sport equipment (or whatever designs you wish) onto the white paper. Cut them out.

3

Use paints to color in the sporting shapes.

If you wish, paint a large white soccer net, or some other design onto the front of the box.

Arrange all the sports shapes around the box and glue them on.

Go Team Elmo! Elmo loves playing sports with his friends. Which sport is Elmo playing today?

Shoe-box aquarium

Make your own under-sea scene, complete with a chest full of sunken treasures. The best thing about these fish is they don't need feeding!

You will need

- 1 empty shoe box
- Acrylic paints and brush
- Scissors
- Blue acetate film cut to the same size as shoe box
- Clear adhesive tape
- White paper and pencil
- Clear thread
- Tissue paper: light and dark green

1

Cut the bottom out of the shoe box, leaving a ¾-inch border all around the edges.

2

Stand the box upright and paint the outside light blue all over. When dry, paint some light green and dark blue streaks over it. Paint the inside floor sandy yellow.

3

Cut the blue acetate film to fit inside the box. Stick it in place with tape.

On white paper, draw and color in with paint a few fish, a starfish, and a treasure chest on a big mound of brown sand. Make sure the mound is big enough to fold over and be used to stand the chest upright. Cut them out.

Using clear adhesive tape, attach clear thread to the fish. Tape the other ends of the thread to the inside top of the box, so the fish look as if they are swimming.

Cut 4 strips from the tissue paper and tape them to the top of the box so they hang down like seaweed. Tape the starfish to the side of the box. Fold over the bottom of the treasure chest and tape the flap to the floor so it stands up on its own.

Elmo is pretending he is swimming in the ocean. What creatures will Elmo see there?

Slithery snail pots

These smiling snails look great and they can store a special surprise. You can hide your tiny treasures under their shell!

You will need

- 5 ounces air-drying clay cut in half
- Plastic knife
- 1 purple pipe cleaner
- Scissors
- Toothpick
- Acrylic paints: red, blue, yellow, purple, black, white
- Paintbrush

1 kids

Roll a ¾-inch ball and 2 tiny balls from half of the clay. Stick the 2 tiny balls onto the larger ball. Cut 2 short pieces of pipe cleaner and push them into the larger ball.

2

With the rest of the clay from the first half, make a tapered oval shape. Use your thumbs to create an indent in the middle. Stick the head to the untapered end.

3

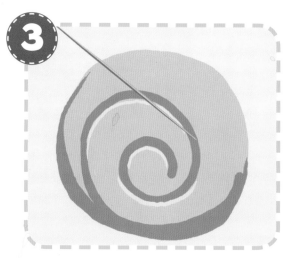

Roll the other half of clay into a ball and shape into a hollow shell shape. Check it fits the base of your model. Add a spiral on each side using the toothpick. Let dry overnight.

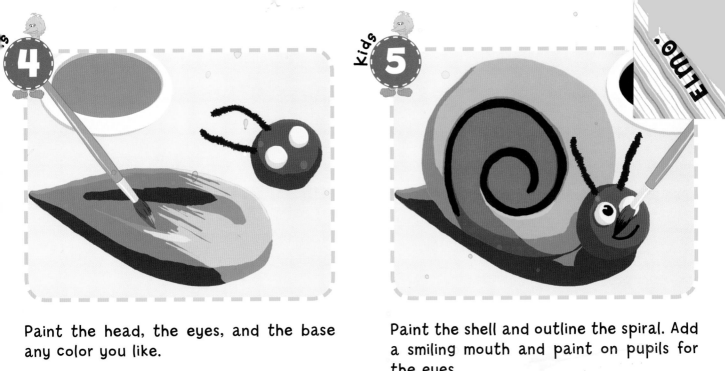

Paint the head, the eyes, and the base any color you like.

Paint the shell and outline the spiral. Add a smiling mouth and paint on pupils for the eyes.

What super treasures will you keep inside your secret snail?

For a grasshopper pot, make a long base and lid and push 6 green pipe-cleaner legs into the base. Paint the pot bright green all over and add red spots.

69

Pet photo frame

If you like animals as much as Elmo does, make this cute frame for a picture of your favorite pet or animal.

You will need

- 4 cardboard strips 6 x 1 inch
- 12 Popsicle sticks
- Cardboard (to fit photo)
- 2 different-sized pens (any kind)
- Acrylic paint
- Photo of pet or favorite animal
- Scissors
- Clear adhesive tape

1

Paint the Popsicle sticks and let dry (or use colored ones).

2

Glue 3 Popsicle sticks onto each cardboard strip, leaving about an inch gap at both ends. Then glue the ends of the cardboard strips together into a frame shape.

3

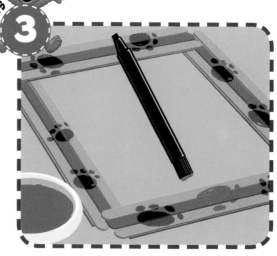

Dip the end of the largest pen into the paint and press down around the frame. Then use the smaller pen to add circles to complete the paw prints.

4

Tape a photo of your pet into the frame then cover the back with a piece of cardboard.

Shell plant pot

The next time you're at the beach, pick up a handful of seashells, or ask your mommy to buy some at a craft store. They make a plain plant pot magic!

You will need

- Seashells
- Acrylic paint
- Paintbrushes
- Clean plant pot (plastic or ceramic)
- White glue and brush

1

Paint some shells in bright colors. Let dry. Paint leaves on the side of a plant pot. Let dry.

2

Glue the shells onto the plant pot. Let the glue dry.

3

Paint snail bodies coming out from under the shells, or create other designs you like around the shells and on the pot.

4

Paint faces and antennae onto the snails, or add other patterns. Let dry. Now add a plant to your pot.

Elmo loves going to the beach and feeling the water splash across his feet! What kind of creatures can you find in the sea?

Racing sailboats

Rub-a-dub! I don't like getting clean but these little boats make washing in the tub more fun.

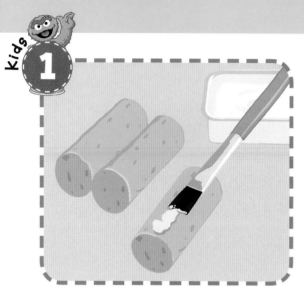

1

Glue the corks together, side by side. Let dry.

You will need

For each boat:
- 3 corks
- White glue and brush
- 2 Popsicle sticks
- Toothpick
- Scraps of colored paper

2

Glue the two Popsicle sticks to the top of the corks as shown. Let dry.

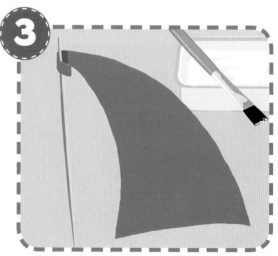

3

Cut a triangular sail from some colored paper. Apply a little glue to the tip of the sail and wrap it around the top of the toothpick mast. Let dry.

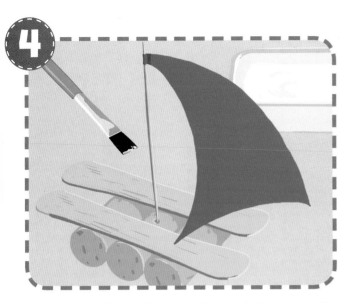

4

Make a hole in the center of the middle cork between the sticks. Push the toothpick mast into the hole. Bend the sail so it sits on the top of the boat.

5

Cut a tiny triangle in yellow paper and glue to the top of the toothpick mast to make a flag.

Rubber Duckie floats in the water, just like these little boats do. Can you name something else that floats in water?

Chocolate nests

Make an Easter treat for the family with yummy chocolate nests. Don't forget to ask an adult to help.

You will need

For 5 nests:
- Heaped ½ cup sugar
- ½ cup butter
- ½ cup cocoa powder
- 2 tablespoons corn syrup
- 2½ ounces shredded wheat
- Aluminum foil
- Medium saucepan
- Wooden spoon
- Mini chocolate eggs or jelly beans

1

Put the sugar, cocoa powder, butter, and corn syrup into the saucepan.

2

Place the pan on a low heat and stir slowly until the mixture melts. Don't let it boil!

kids 3

Let the mixture cool slightly. Crumble the shredded wheat into the mixture and stir until the shredded wheat is covered.

ABBY

Make the aluminum foil into five bowl shapes. Add some mixture and press down in the middle to make nest shapes. Put them in the fridge to cool and set.

When the nests are fully set, remove the foil and fill the chocolate nests with the mini chocolate eggs.

I wonder how big these delicious chocolate nests would need to be to hold me?

Pretty plant labels

If you have lots of plants in pots in your garden, you can use these cute tags to help you remember their names. Plants and flowers are so magical!

You will need

★ Felt-tip pen
★ Colored craft foam
★ Scissors
★ Pipe cleaners
★ White glue and brush
★ Googly eyes
★ Popsicle sticks

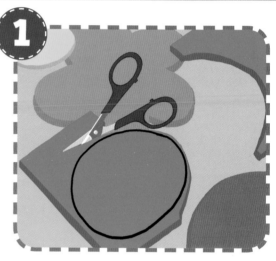

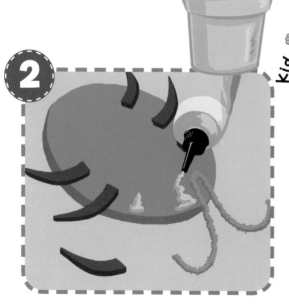

1

With a felt-tip pen, draw some simple shapes, such as a ladybug, a flower, or a tomato on pieces of colored craft foam. Cut them out.

kids

2

Use smaller foam shapes or pipe cleaners to create butterfly antennae or ladybug legs. Glue in place and let dry.

3

Glue on some googly eyes, if you wish; let dry. Glue each shape onto a Popsicle stick.

Push your labels into plant pots, seed trays or your garden. Ask an adult to write the name of the plant on the label.

Did you know that tomatoes are actually fruit not vegetables? What's your favorite fruit?

Chest of drawers

Bert has created this chest to tidy up a lot of little things, from paper clips to stamps. Me? I prefer messes.

You will need

- 6 empty matchboxes
- White glue and brush
- Selection of old/used stamps
- Scissors
- 6 brass paper fasteners

1 Glue 3 matchboxes together on top of one another. Do the same with the remaining 3 matchboxes.

2 Glue the 2 sets of matchboxes together side by side. Let dry.

kids **3** Remove the drawers. Use the end of a small pair of scissors to make a hole in the middle of each drawer. Push a paper fastener into each hole and bend the ends to fix them in place.

Paint the backs of the stamps with glue and stick them on the matchboxes. Overlap the stamps and stick them on at different angles to make a fun design.

Trim the stamps where they overlap the edges of the box. Put the drawers back inside the boxes.

I love spending time with my paperclip collection. What will you keep in your chest of drawers?

Bread dough animals

Elmo loves the smell of fresh baked bread. Uncooked bread is called dough. It's easy to make shapes with bread dough, like these animal shapes.

You will need

- Mixing bowl
- 1 packet active dry yeast
- ⅔ cup warm water
- 1 teaspoon salt
- 1 teaspoon sugar
- ¼ cup unsalted butter
- 1 cup flour
- Raisins

1

Kids 2

In a mixing bowl, dissolve the yeast in the warm water. Stir in the salt and sugar, then add the flour and butter.

With your hands, make a ball with the dough and knead it for 5 minutes, or until the dough feels smooth and stretchy.

Divide the dough into 3 or 4 smaller pieces and shape into animals, such as a snail, a turtle, a fish, and a snake. Push raisins into the dough for eyes.

Place the animal shapes onto a baking sheet, then leave the dough to rise in a warm place for 30 minutes. Bake in the oven for 20 minutes at 350°F until golden in color. Leave to cool, then enjoy your tasty animal snacks.

Snails and turtles have hard shells. Can you think of any other creatures that have shells?

Bottle garden

If you'd like a garden but you don't have much room, this bottle garden is perfect. Just remember to water it once a week and your plants will be happy.

You will need

★★ Large glass jar with lid
★★ Clear adhesive tape
★★ Old spoon
★★ Cotton ball
★★ 2 wooden skewers
★★ Colored gravel
★★ Soil mix
★★ Small plants

Make your bottle garden more interesting with a tropical bird on a stick from a garden center. Now scram!

1

Start by taping the spoon to a wooden skewer, using lots of adhesive tape. This is for digging. Make a cleaning tool by taping a cotton ball to the other skewer.

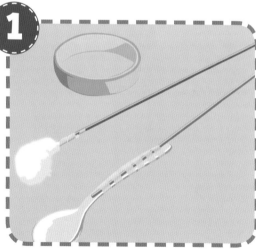

2

Spoon about 1½ inches of colored gravel into the bottom of the jar.

3

Now add about 3 inches of moist soil mix and press it down with your hands.

4

Use the spoon to make a hole in the soil mix. Add one of the plants and press the soil down firmly around its base. Add more plants in the same way.

5

Dip the cotton ball in water and squeeze it out. Use your cleaning tool to wipe away any smears of soil mix from the sides of the jar.

Paper pom-poms

Make your presents look really special with paper pom-pom decorations. Go pom-pom crazy with me!

You will need

- 2 sheets of tissue paper in different shades of the same color
- Scissors
- White glue and brush

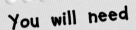

1

Cut out 2 strips about an inch wide from each sheet of colored tissue paper.

2

Brush glue along the bottom edge of each strip and glue all 4 strips together.

3

Use scissors to snip along the strips, making each cut about ½ inch apart. Don't cut all the way through.

ELMO'S

Spread glue along the bottom of the strip and roll the shape up. Press it together at the bottom and let dry.

Use your fingers to fluff out the pom-pom. Dab some glue on the bottom and stick on top of a present.

I'm going to make my pom-pom from recycled paper. Or you can make a pom-pom using shimmery foil paper and pinking shears for a spiky look.

87

Dinosaur forest

Elmo is using his imagination. He is pretending this "swampy" forest is a mini-world of adventure and discovery.

You will need

- Large plastic pan or tray
- Various vegetable tops (carrots, turnips, parsnips, beets, and pineapples)
- Water
- Toy dinosaurs

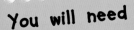

1

Cut the tops off some vegetables and fill the plastic plate or tray with a shallow layer of water.

2 kids

Float the vegetable tops on the water with the cut edges down.

3 kids

Set the pan or tray in a warm place. Wait for about 2 weeks for the shoots and leaves to sprout. Make sure to keep water in the pan at all times.

4

Dinosaurs lived on Earth about 230 million years ago. That's a long time ago!

ABBY'S CADABBY'S GAR

After the leaves are tall enough, arrange your toy dinosaurs in the floating forest and make up a fun story about them.

Magical watering can

Plants and flowers need sun, soil, and water. I've painted a funny face on my watering can. Why don't you give it a try, too?

You will need

- Pencil
- Plain metal watering can
- Acrylic paints
- Paintbrushes

1

Make sure the watering can is clean and dry. Use a pencil to mark out a design, like this flowery face using the spout as the nose.

2 kids

Paint on the face and petals, or other designs you have created. Let dry.

3 kids

Add another coat of paint if necessary. Let dry.

4

Add patterns around the face, handles, or spout. Let dry thoroughly.

You'll love watering your flowers with this pretty can.

Kitty photo album

This collage photo album will make a purr-fect present for your favorite cat lover!

You will need

- 6 sheets 8½ x 11 inches, colored cardboard
- Scraps of card in orange, white, pink, green, black, and blue
- Hole punch
- Pinking shears
- White glue and brush
- 3-foot long piece of green cord

Pile together the 6 sheets of colored cardboard with the cover sheet on top. Punch 2 holes on the left-hand side.

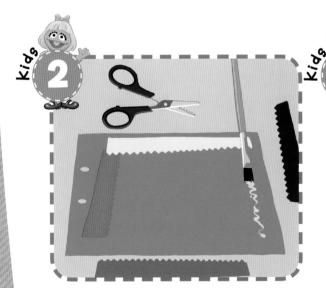

Using the pinking shears cut a strip from each of the card scraps. Arrange them to make a border on the cover and glue in place.

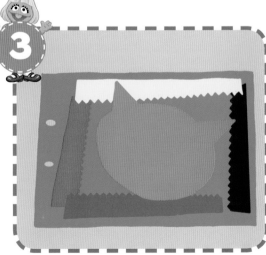

Draw and cut out a large cat face from orange cardboard. Glue it on the cover, overlapping the borders as shown.

4 Draw and cut out the cat's oval white eyes with green and black pupils. Cut out a pink nose, mouth, some ears, and black whiskers. Arrange these on the face and glue them in place.

5 Thread the length of cord through the holes, starting from the back and including all the pages. Tie in a bow at the front. Knot the ends of the cord to stop them from fraying.

Instead of an orange kitty, make a photo album with a picture of your pet on the front. Or, just make a pretty design any way you wish!

Scented hangings

Hang these fragrant little butterflies in your clothes chest or closet and your clothing will always smell fresh. They make great gifts, too!

You will need

- Salt-dough mixture
- Rolling pin
- Butterfly-shaped cookie cutter
- Toothpick
- Ribbon
- Baking sheet
- Acrylic paint and paintbrushes
- Lavender essential oil

1 Make the salt dough, using the recipe at the start of the book. Roll it out to a thickness of about ¾ inch.

kids

2 Using a cookie cutter, cut shapes out of the dough. Make a hole at the top of each shape with the toothpick.

Put the shapes on a cookie sheet and bake in a pre-heated oven at 250°F for about 3 hours. Let cool.

Paint the shapes, leaving a small square on the back unpainted.

My mommy told me that lavender oil helps people to feel relaxed, so hang a butterfly over your bed. You'll soon be having sweet dreams!

Add a few drops of lavender essential oil to the unpainted area. Thread a ribbon through the hole and knot it at the back.

Heart-shaped hangings make a great Valentine's day gift for a special friend!